D0598398

FIDM | THE ~~FASHION~~ ~~IN~~ STITUTE OF
DESIGN & ~~MERCHA~~ NDISING

759.4
M746

20000524

MONET

759.4 M746   c. 1

FIDM - SF

1. **RETURN BOOKS ON DUE DATE:**
   A fine is charged for each day a book is overdue excluding weekends and holidays.

2. **REPORT A LOST BOOK AT ONCE:**
   The charge for a lost book equals the replacement value and handling cost.

3. **PREVENT DAMAGE:**
   A charge is made for any damage to the book.

LS 1146-R1285

THE HISTORY AND TECHNIQUES
OF THE GREAT MASTERS

MONET

THE HISTORY AND TECHNIQUES
OF THE GREAT MASTERS

MONET

Trewin Copplestone

Fashion Institute of Design & Merchandising
Resource & Research Center
55 Stockton St., 5th Floor
San Francisco, CA 94108-5805

CHARTWELL
BOOKS, INC.

A QUARTO BOOK

Published by Chartwell Books
A Division of Book Sales, Inc.
110 Enterprise Avenue
Secaucus, New Jersey 07094

Copyright © 1987 Quarto Publishing plc
All rights reserved. No part of this publication
may be reproduced, stored in a retrieval system
or transmitted in any form or by any means,
electronic, mechanical, photocopying, recording
or otherwise, without the permission of the
copyright holder

ISBN 1-55521-212-3

This book was designed and produced by
Quarto Publishing plc
The Old Brewery, 6 Blundell Street

London N7 9BH

Senior Editor Polly Powell
Art Editor Vincent Murphy

Project Editor Hazel Harrison
Designer Terry Smith
Picture Researcher Celestine Dars

Art Director Moira Clinch
Editorial Director Carolyn King

Many thanks to Bob Cocker and Paul Swain

Typeset by QV Typesetting Ltd

Manufactured in Hong Kong by Regent
Publishing Services Limited
Printed in Hong Kong by Leefung-Asco
Printers Ltd

CONTENTS

THE PAINTINGS

INTRODUCTION

CAROLUS-DURAN
Portrait of Claude Monet
1867
Musée Marmottan, Paris

Monet's paintings carry a peculiar magic. They are ordinary enough in subject matter, consisting almost exclusively of basically direct treatments of landscape — figures rarely appear, and after 1890 not at all. The paintings have little obvious drama or planned appeal to the emotions, and they make no kind of political or social statement. Nevertheless they evoke a constant delight from most viewers, and this very delight in many ways obscures Monet's really extraordinary achievement. It could be claimed that Monet, more than any of the Impressionists, opened the path to a new understanding of the nature of painting.

At first sight Monet appears as an uncomplicated, non-intellectual painter, constantly excited by the world around him, drawing his subjects from nothing more ambitious than his local countryside, and dedicated to exploring the effects of light on the natural landscape. We think of him as a simple, direct person leading a quiet life and blessed with an equable temperament, unbeset by any of the tensions and anxieties that afflicted painters such as Van Gogh and Gauguin. He seems to personify, not just the "happy painter" but also the nature of the Impressionist movement itself, and indeed it was one of his paintings, *Impression, Sunrise* (see page 27), exhibited at the First Impressionist Exhibition in 1874, that gave the movement its name. (The word "impressionist" was in fact intended as a derisory comment, but was taken by most of the group as an acceptable description of its aims.)

In fact Monet's main characteristics were determination and single-mindedness, and his nature was much more complex than his paintings would lead us to believe. His life was a constant struggle with what he saw as insoluble technical problems, and he was frequently so dissatisfied with his work that he would not allow it to be taken from the studio. In his home life he was an autocrat, demanding total punctuality from both his family and his servants. With his friends he was more relaxed, and he enjoyed parties and the café life that was such an important part of the Parisian artistic scene. Although a Parisian from commercial necessity, he always loved the countryside, which he treasured for its infinite variety as well as for the solitude it offered. The landscape, and particularly the sea coast and water, was his passion throughout his life.

But passion is not really the word that provides the key to either the Impressionist movement as a whole or to Monet in particular. Perhaps the most significant thread running through the movement and unifying its varied strands is a concern with vision rather than with emotion or social statement. When Degas painted his laundresses he was not concerned, as Dickens would have been, with the sweatshop conditions in which they worked, but with colors and the effects of light on sharply pressed, clean fabrics. Similarly, it would be unwise to assume that because Monet painted the façade of Rouen Cathedral many times it was because of any strong attachment to the faith it embodied.

Despite the absence of dramatic, emotional and social involvement on the part of its central figures, the Impressionist movement initiated a great artistic revolution, and one that has had a lasting effect, not only on artists, but also on the art-aware public. It changed all the ideas of what constitutes a painting, distinguishing, in effect, between a "picture" and a "painting." Any appreciation of what the movement achieved hinges on an understanding of Monet's own achievement; he was its pivot and its center, and his long life documents its development and evolution well into our own century.

Monet's intention, developed over his entire painting career, was to paint what he saw. This may seem to us a straightforward, even commonplace ambition, but it is important to realize that it was far from being a universal preoccupation of artists of the past, nor is it often a primary concern of artists today. In Monet's own time the well-known academic painters were concerned, not with painting what they saw, but with producing highly finished, often idealized works with a social or religious message, and it was the Impressionists' emphasis on vision that not only distinguished them but gave rise to the hostility and ridicule that greeted their first public appearance.

The simple presentation of landscape or still life was regarded in the nineteenth century as an inferior, if attractive, form of painting, although the beginnings of a change could be discerned with such painters as Constable and Turner in England and the Barbizon school of painters in France. However, even though these painters exerted a considerable influence on the Impressionists they were less concerned with color and light than with tone and form; even Eugène Boudin, Monet's first mentor, built his open-air paintings on a tonal base, seeing his forms in terms of light and dark rather than of color. The Impressionsts, on the other hand, saw the whole of nature in terms of color and light: color was everywhere, even in the deepest shadows, which traditionally had been rendered simply as dark brown or gray. This preoccupation with color made their paintings quite startlingly different from any that had gone before, and no one was more determined in the pursuit of color than Monet himself.

The struggle to record nature

Monet came up against one essential problem presented by the observation of nature: the constant changes caused both by an ever-moving light source and by the movement of the forms themselves — clouds, trees, grasses and water were perpetually in flux. What he saw never stayed the same long enough for the painting of it. For an artist dedicated to painting what he saw the challenge was relentless, and the problem ultimately insoluble.

Thus Monet's apparently commonplace ambition was actually a much greater task than it seems, and it caused him both mental anguish and physical exhaus-

CLAUDE MONET
Regatta at Argenteuil
1872, Musée d'Orsay, Paris

Monet's painting during his settled life at Argenteuil has a particular joy, freshness and visual delight, reflecting his pleasure in the small town and surrounding country, especially the river. This painting, a small *esquisse*, or preliminary sketch, is constructed of broad directional, form-following brushstrokes creating the impression of sunlight with great immediacy. The luminosity of color and the flat patterning both show the influence of Japanese prints, of which Monet owned many at this time. The painting was almost certainly bought by his friend Gustave Caillebotte, a rich collector and painter who exhibited in the Impressionist Group Exhibitions.

tion. Also, however, it transformed his paintings from the hard, Japanese-print-like shapes of his early works such as *Women in a Garden* (see page 19) to the evanescent, ethereal images of the water gardens in the late *Nymphéas* (*Waterlilies*) panels (see page 57).

As his studies and experiments advanced, Monet perceived a further, even more daunting complication. In consciously attempting to paint what he saw, he was actually seeing himself observing the changes of light, and thus was chasing not what he had seen but what he himself had retained of what he had seen. He could never catch up with himself.

CLAUDE MONET
The Bank at Gennevilliers
About 1870, Private collection

Gennevilliers was a small town on the opposite side of the river from Argenteuil, the two being linked by a bridge.

This small sketch, almost certainly done rapidly on the spot, presages the bold brushwork of *Rue Montorgeuil* (opposite), particularly in the treatment of the path, though this was painted at a much earlier date.

But during the process he unconsciously made the most far-reaching discovery of all. His vision, which permitted him only to translate a sensation of color to the canvas, was not spatial but flat, but in spite of this a spatial element did appear on the canvas. By the time he had begun work on the *Waterlilies* paintings the problem had been compounded by the surface of the water he was painting, which was both visually present and transparent. So where was the canvas surface — under the water, on its surface, or in the air space in between?

Monet's painting from 1872, when he settled at Argenteuil (near Paris on the banks of the Seine) onwards, could be seen as the presentation of the direct sketch from nature as the finished work. From this period until his death his basic method was established. Although in his later paintings representationalism and the clear delination of volume became less important, he continued the brush and paint application he had learned when painting with Renoir, Pissarro and other artist friends. Energetic and varied, his technique

ranged from heavy impastos built up in short, jabbed strokes to long, thick "drawn" brushstrokes. His color was broken into small, fluttering areas where dense foliage was being described, or tense, long, thin or broad strokes where water or sky was treated. He was not a technician by temperament, but his painting methods were marvelously appropriate to his needs.

The artist's early life

Monet's early life was beset by the usual lack of recognition and attendant financial problems, but unlike Van Gogh he did not remain unrecognized, and was relatively affluent when he died in 1926. Although his early life had been disrupted by the great social and political upheavals of late nineteenth-century France, he played little part in them. Throughout the First World War he remained in his house at Giverny, and the great artistic movements of the early twentieth century, Fauvism, Cubism, Futurism and Surrealism, completely passed him by; when Monet died, Picasso was forty-five and already famous.

Claude Monet was born in 1840, the son of a successful wholesale grocer in Paris who moved with his family to Le Havre when Claude was five. He grew up there and was conscripted into the army in 1861, being sent to Algeria but invalided out the following year.

He had already begun to paint before his conscription, and was introduced to open-air painting by the seascape painter Eugène Boudin, whose canvases have a fresh directness, with great luminous sweeps of sky. At the same time he met the Dutch landscape painter J.B. Jongkind, and it was not long before he decided that he wished to become a professional painter. His father somewhat reluctantly agreed to support him provided he studied in the *atelier* of a reputable academic artist in Paris, and accordingly he joined Charles Gleyre's academy in 1862. Some academics gave little or no attention to their students, but Gleyre's reputation was high and he had many students, among whom at the time were Bazille, Sisley and Renoir.

Frédéric Bazille was Monet's first close friend in the art world, and his studio was the focus for a group of young painters from Gleyre's academy who were impatient with the academic processes and teaching methods. They were also dismayed by the commercial ambitions they encountered in the official painting world, where success was more important than achievement, and reputation than quality of work.

Monet and his friends left Gleyre's when it closed in 1864, but Monet, still attracted by the idea of painting in

CLAUDE MONET
Rue Montorgeuil:
Fête Nationale
1887, Musée d'Orsay, Paris

In his series of paintings of the *Gare Saint-Lazare* (see page 35) Monet had begun to handle paint and color in a way that made the paint surface itself the subject of the painting, with figures and details often described with just a flick of the brush. This is one of a series of paintings of Paris done in 1887 in which this concept was taken even further; here the individual details, such as figures and flags, are seen as a pattern of inter-relating verticals, diagonals and areas of color.

the open air, stayed in Paris and painted in the nearby countryside or on the Normandy coast. At the same time he began living with Camille Doncieux, and in 1867 she bore a son, Jean. This was a lean period for Monet, and when he and Camille finally found themselves penniless he was forced to return home to Le Havre.

In 1870 Monet and Camille were married in Paris, but in autumn of the same year the Franco-Prussian war broke out, and this was to have a dramatic effect on

French cultural life, particularly in the aftermath of the siege of Paris. The young painters working in and around Paris were dispersed, and Bazille was killed in a futile engagement early in the war. Degas joined the National Guard and participated in the siege of Paris, but Monet took Camille and Jean on their honeymoon, after which they went to London, avoiding both war and siege. In 1871 they returned to France and settled in Argenteuil.

Argenteuil is now a suburb of Paris, but then it was a charming country town sufficiently close to Paris to provide the twin benefits of café life and the delights of the countryside and river banks. It became Monet's home for the next six years as well as a home from home for his artist friends, among whom was Renoir, who often stayed with Monet and frequently painted the same subjects as they sat together on the river bank. These paintings were the real beginnings of Impressionism, and this was one of the most formative periods of Monet's art as well as one of the happiest in his life.

New beginnings

It was also a period of great expansion and prosperity in France, in the aftermath of the Franco-Prussian war. During the 1870s the country, and particularly Paris, established the artistic pre-eminence which it was to hold right up to the Second World War. The feeling of a

CLAUDE MONET
*The Seine at Porte-Villez;
Winter, Snow*
1885, Private collection

The river and its different moods was a source of endless fascination for Monet, and here the effects of snow and icy water are captured with singular effectiveness. The earlier form-following brush strokes seen in *Regatta at*

Argenteuil (see page 7) have now given way to the *tache* method of building the painting. A darker laying in of thin green-brown underpainting is covered with a thick white, near white or blue dashes of dry paint. The warmest color is in the house behind the trees and the strongest is found in small touches of cobalt blue in the water.

new beginning was heightened by the rebuilding of Paris which had been carried out during the 1860s at considerable expense. All signs of past conflict were obliterated, and a new age had dawned, not only in art but in literature, with such names as Victor Hugo, Flaubert, Balzac, George Sand, Stendhal and de Maupassant leading an impressive rollcall.

When we look at Monet's work during this period it becomes obvious that the old academic tradition represented by such artists as Gleyre and Adolphe Bougereau were no longer relevant to the new creative energy. Undoubtedly society was not conscious of new needs — it seldom is — but the needs were there, and Impressionism, with its directness and immediacy, was able to fill them, at least after the first shock of unfamiliarity had worn off.

At this time the important annual art exhibition in Paris was the Salon, which had opened in the seventeenth century to exhibit the works of the newly formed French Academy. By the nineteenth century the Salon had become so restrictive that even to exhibit was difficult for a non-Academician (so many were rejected that in 1863 a Salon des Refusés was inaugurated as a short-lived alternative). Nevertheless, all young and aspiring painters wished to exhibit, since not only did it bring public recognition, it was also the best marketplace, and Monet was no exception. In 1865 he had been accepted with two seascapes (which he appears to have sold), and a year later a portrait of Camille and a landscape were also hung. But despite this *succès d'estime* he was rarely able to sell his work and often had to rely on funding from his father and his friends.

A change came in 1870 when Monet met Paul Durand-Ruel in London, where both had taken refuge from the war. Durand-Ruel was a picture dealer, one of a newly developing breed of sophisticated and well-educated men who appreciated good paintings, bought them themselves, and were able to persuade potential buyers of their worth. Hitherto, picture dealing had been largely a sideline for shopkeepers selling artists' materials, stationery and so on, and they were little interested in the quality of the works they sold. Durand-Ruel became the most important supporter of the Impressionists during the 1870s and 1880s, and Monet was one of his most successful painters. By the end of the century other dealers had become interested, and Monet and the other Impressionists could afford to ignore the Salon route to success.

Sadly, in 1873, Durand-Ruel found himself in financial straits and was forced to stop buying, causing prob-

CLAUDE MONET
Suzanne Private collection

Although pastels did not form a large part of Monet's body of work, he produced a number of them, both early and late in his career, finding the medium well suited to his self-imposed task of capturing rapid impressions. This portrait, done in the Giverny period, is of Suzanne Hoschedé, Alice's daughter. In 1892 she married an American painter, Theodore Butler, but became ill after the birth of a child and died in 1899, causing great grief to Monet and his wife.

lems for Monet too. However, at much the same time Monet struck up a friendship with an apparently wealthy businessman, Ernest Hoschedé, and his wife Alice, and the relationship was to have a long-term effect on his life. For the present, it gave him some income from sales to Hoschedé, as well as loans from him.

Monet's life at Argenteuil with Camille and his son provided the stability of a settled household, enabling him to concentrate on the development of his art. In 1874 he became one of the organizers of the First Impressionist Exhibition. Called the "Société Anonyme des Artistes, Peintres, Sculpteurs et Graveurs," the group held its first show in Paris in the studio of the photographer Nadar. The critic Louis Leroy attacked it, suggesting in his article that a "real" (i.e. academic) painter would be driven mad by the works to be seen. Subsequent reviews of other group shows were no more favorable. Another critic, Ballou, reviewing the work of Monet and Cézanne in 1877, wrote: "They provoke laughter and are altogether lamentable. They show the most profound ignorance of design, composition and color. Children amusing themselves with paper and paint could do much better."

But in spite of the poor reception the group shows became an annual event, and Monet exhibited in the first four, the seventh and the last, after which he had "arrived," and was able to sell his work and arrange one-man shows whenever he wished.

His domestic life was again disrupted when in 1877 Ernest Hoschedé became bankrupt. The two families decided to pool their resources, and they moved to Vetheuil, also on the Seine but considerably further — forty miles — from Paris. Monet managed to keep a small *pied à terre* in Paris to show his paintings, since he could not bring his customers so far from the capital.

The Giverny years

Soon after their arrival at Vetheuil Camille, who had recently borne a second son, Michel, died. Monet became distraught and was unable to work. Alice Hoschedé looked after Monet's children as well as her own six, and the families remained linked, moving together first to Poissy and then to Giverny in 1883. While they were still at Poissy, Ernest Hoschedé, disenchanted with poverty

JOHN SINGER SARGENT
Monet Painting on the Edge of a Wood
1885/7, Tate Gallery, London

Monet became friendly with Sargent after they met at Durand-Ruel's gallery around 1884/5, and Sargent became a regular guest at Giverny in the later 1880s. The two artists painted together in the open air during this period, and this direct sketch, showing all Sargent's considerable virtuosity, is a most convincing impression of Monet at work. The other seated figure is probably Blanche, Monet's daughter-in-law, who often carried his equipment and was his most attentive assistant.

MONET'S PAINTING METHODS

In Morning at Etretat *Monet used a gray-tinted canvas, here visible through the thinly applied paint in the shore area.*

In paintings such as Rue Montorgeuil *Monet has used his brushstrokes to form a vibrating pattern of verticals and diagonals.*

This detail of the foreground of Grain Stacks *shows how Monet saw each area as composed of many different colors of the same tonal value.*

Monet usually painted on standard-sized canvases with a white priming, a break from earlier tradition, in which forms and tones had been built up from dark to light on a dark-toned ground. However, although he said in 1920 that he "always insisted on painting on white canvases, in order to establish on them my scale of values," this statement is not entirely true; in fact he used a wide range of mid-toned primings, often a warm beige or light gray. From about 1860 the color of these primings became an element in the paintings, with small areas either being left unpainted or very lightly covered.

Monet always stood up to work, whether outdoors or in the studio, and he never believed his paintings were finished, frequently reworking them in the studio in spite of his often-stated belief in instantaneity. Except in the earlier works he did little or no underdrawing or tonal underpainting, beginning each painting with colors approximating to the finished ones, and working all over the canvas at the same time with long thin bristle brushes. His brushwork varied from painting to painting as well as through the course of his long career, but one of the main characteristics of his work, and of other members of the group, is the use of what is known as the *tache*, the method of applying paint in small opaque touches, premixed on the palette with the minimum of mixing medium. This provides a patchwork-like fabric of all-over color, described by Zola as "as ensemble of delicate, accurate *taches* which, from a few steps back, give a striking relief to the picture."

The colors shown here, plus lead white, are those used in Bathing at La Grenouillère *(see page 23), and are typical of Monet's palette at the time. In early paintings he also used black, and it is probable that he sometimes extended his range with yellow ocher, burnt sienna and ultramarine.*

1 White; 2 Chrome yellow; 3 Lemon yellow; 4 Vermilion; 5 Prussian blue; 6 Cobalt blue; 7 Emerald green; 8 Viridian; 9 Chrome green; 10 Cobalt violet

and provincial family life, gradually disengaged himself and took up a bachelor life in Paris, where he built up a new business from the sale of a few paintings he had managed to keep.

The move to Giverny coincided with the death of Manet, and Monet went to Paris to be a pallbearer, but his close association with the city was now over, and Giverny became the focus of his life and the subject-source of most of his later paintings. He had purchased a farm-

house on the outskirts of the village, which is about fifty miles from Paris on the banks of the Seine. The house was close to the river and set in water meadows, and here Monet made the water garden that became the subject of his last great paintings. He gradually became isolated from his friends, a semi-recluse.

Ernest's desertion of the family had created a somewhat unconventional situation in the household, since Alice had remained to look after the children. Neither of them was happy about it: Monet was deeply conventional in such matters and Alice was devoutly religious, so for some time there was an undercurrent of tension in the Giverny establishment. However, in 1892 Ernest died, and a quiet wedding ceremony took place.

All the reports of Monet's life at Giverny — and there were many because by this time he was famous and the subject of considerable public interest — reflect the image of a complex and moody man whose humors affected the whole household. He was irascible and

CLAUDE MONET
Blanche painting
1892, Private collection

Blanche Hoschedé, Monet's daughter-in-law, became quite a competent painter under his instruction and often accompanied him on local painting trips. On this one they were joined by another painting friend, probably Caillebotte. The woman in the background is probably Blanche, whose figure was repeated while she took a break from her own painting — a little joke perhaps. This was a private study, and unusual in that Monet rarely painted figures after the 1880s. It shows a good deal of overworking in the head and near arm, and there is less of the fluid assurance which he shows in his landscapes.

unbearable when thwarted, particularly when the weather prevented him from painting — and would sometimes stay in bed all day refusing any attention. He was only forty-three when he bought the house, with exactly half his life still to live, yet he had already become an autocratic patriarch, and clearly fostered the image. Altogether, he lived exactly as he wished, with scant respect for the wishes and needs of others; for instance, he forbade the marriage of Alice's daughter Germaine to Pierre Sisley, the painter's son, on the grounds that Pierre's occupation, as an inventor, was too insecure. Odd behavior from a once-impoverished painter, one might think.

The planning and development of his garden became his major preoccupation and demanded much of the not inconsiderable income he was now making from his painting. Six gardeners were employed, one of whom looked after the water garden exclusively. This, filled with a great variety of waterlilies and surrounded by willows, was developed from the purchase of some nearby land, and across its narrower part Monet constructed a Japanese bridge he had designed himself, based on a Japanese print he had bought in the 1860s.

Monet's house and garden became a place of pilgrimage for friends and admirers. In spite of his reclusive tendencies, friends still played a part in his life and he was deeply distressed as one by one they died, suffering periods of fierce melancholy which prevented him from working. The gravest blow of all was the death of Alice in May 1911, and he did not work until the end of the year.

The most important friend of his late years, and one who survived him, was Georges Clemenceau, the statesman and journalist, whose support during the time after Alice's death was crucial. But Monet's troubles were not over; he had begun to suffer from failing eyesight some years before the loss of Alice, but it was not until 1912 that he was persuaded to see an eye specialist, who diagnosed a double cataract, requiring an operation. Fearing both the operation and its effect on his vision, Monet refused, and even Clemenceau could not persuade him. (He did finally have the operation, in 1923.)

The last great works

Yet another blow for Monet was the death of his older son Jean in 1914 just before the outbreak of war. Jean's widow, Blanche, one of Alice's daughters, came to live with him and cared for him for the rest of his life. She was also a painter, and they often painted together.

Blanche and Clemenceau formed a mutually suppor-

CLAUDE MONET
A Shady Walk
1920, Private collection

Monet created, as part of his garden at Giverny, a walk from the main entrance to the farmhouse itself, which included about six arched pergolas. He liked a controlled wildness, and as time passed this walk became a riot of color, with flowers spreading across the path itself to produce the effect of a shaded, multi-colored grotto. This late painting, done when his eyesight had so deteriorated that he could see the swirling motion of color but few distinct forms, is probably of this walk; he rarely left his garden in his last years. The work is a moving expression of his devotion to his painting, and constitutes a triumph of experience over physical limitation.

tive alliance, and it was through Clemenceau that Monet's last great commission was secured, for the panels known as the *Nymphéas*, or *Waterlilies* (see page 57) destined to decorate a specially constructed room in the Orangerie, Paris. Clemenceau was devoted to Monet and continued to visit him up to his death, though there were, of course, strains in their relationship, mainly caused by Monet's failure to meet his deadlines. His dissatisfaction with his work, partly the result of his failing vision, prompted violent physical attacks on his work, including the *Nymphéas* panels, which he altered constantly. He would not allow them to leave the studio, and there was a real danger that he might even destroy them, since it was his habit to make bonfires in the garden of paintings that he found inadequate. The panels were not, in fact, put in place until the year after Monet's death.

Clemenceau was present at Giverny on December 5th, 1926 when, around noon, Monet died. As he had wished, he was given a quiet funeral, with Clemenceau and the painters Pierre Bonnard, K-X Roussel and Edouard Vuillard as pallbearers.

CHRONOLOGY OF MONET'S LIFE

1840   November 4th: Claude Oscar Monet born Paris. Auguste Rodin born in same year.

1845   Family moves to Le Havre.

c.1856/7 Meets Eugène Boudin.

1859   First visit to Paris; meets a number of painters including Pissarro.

1861-2   Military service in Algeria. Discharged because of ill health. Meets Dutch painter Jongkind.

1862   Enters Gleyre's studio where he meets Bazille, Renoir and Sisley.

1864   Leaves Gleyre's studio. Paints at Fontainebleau.

1865   Shares studio with Bazille in Paris. First exhibits at Salon.

1866   Portrait of Camille success at Salon.

1867   First son Jean born. Financial problems force him to return to family in Le Havre.

1868   Lives with Camille Doncieux at Etretat during winter.

1870   Marries Camille. Outbreak of Franco-Prussian war causes visit to England where he meets Durand-Ruel.

1871   Returns to France and settles at Argenteuil. Rejected by Royal Academy, London.

1872-4   Durand-Ruel buys paintings.

1874   First Impressionist Exhibition.

1876   Meets Hoschedé family.

1877   Ernest Hoschedé becomes bankrupt. Works in Paris on *Gare Saint-Lazare* paintings.

1878   Moves to Ventheuil and is joined by the Hoschedé family. Second son Michel is born.

1879   Camille dies. Alice Hoschedé takes charge of household.

1880   Exhibits at Salon.

Impression, Sunrise

Boats at Etretat

Grain Stacks, End of Summer

Poplars on the Banks of the Epte

1881   Moves to Poissy. Durand-Ruel resumes purchase of work after earlier financial problems.

1882   Exhibits in seventh group exhibition.

1883   Moves to Giverny. One-man show at Durand-Ruel gallery. Summer: makes first paintings of Giverny region. Trips to the Midi and Italian Riviera with Renoir. Visits Cézanne during trip.

1884-7   Paints at Giverny and northern French coast.

1888   Paints at Antibes. Refuses Legion d'Honneur.

1889   Exhibits with Rodin at Georges Petits gallery. Organizes private subscription list to purchase Manet's *Olympia* for the State.

1890   Begins "series" paintings with *Grain Stacks*. Purchases home at Giverny.

1892   Begins *Rouen* series. Marries Alice Hoschedé.

1893   Begins making water garden.

1895   Painting trip to Norway.

1896   *Early morning on Seine* series.

1899   Begins first paintings of water garden and Japanese bridge. Painting trip to London.

1900-1   Works on *Thames* series in London.

1903   Begins second *Water Garden* series.

1908   Painting journey (last) to Venice. Trouble with eyesight.

1911   Death of Alice.

1914   Builds new studio for *Waterlilies* panels. Death of son Jean.

1921   Deterioration in his sight..

1922   Bequest of *Waterlilies* to state.

1923   Has cataract operation, which is partially successful.

1926   December 5th: death at Giverny.

THE PAINTINGS

WOMEN IN THE GARDEN

1866/7
100¾×81¾in/256×208cm
Oil on canvas
Musée d'Orsay, Paris

Monet planned this painting as a major exhibition piece for the Salon of 1867. The Salon was still at this time the place where artistic reputations were made, and no young artist could afford to ignore it. Monet had previously shown small works in the manner of Boudin and a full-length portrait of his wife Camille, but this painting, a very large-scale work more than eight feet high, was clearly intended as a publicity work designed to gain commissions, and the size of the signature suggests that Monet wanted to fix his name in the mind of the public.

The work, however, was rejected, which perhaps did not surprise Monet unduly; since his time at Gleyre's studio he had had no very high regard for academic judgement. Although the painting might have appeared to conform to the pattern of figure composition that was acceptable to the Academicians it lacked one important element: the figures in the group have no dramatic relationship with each other, that is, there is no "story line" in the painting. This was then regarded as the *raison d'être* of a painting, whether it be historical, literary, religious or social, but in Monet's work the people simply exist. Also they all look somewhat alike — not surprising, as Camille posed for all of them.

But this was not the only reason for the rejection of the painting. Monet's technique itself left much to be desired in terms of academic practice. As in other early works the paint handling is close to that of Manet, with the shapes of the figures, the shadows and the foliage clearly defined, and little range of tonal modeling. This treatment may well have reminded the judges of the public scandals caused by Manet's work, first by the *Déjeuner sur l'Herbe* displayed in the Salon des Refusés in 1863 and then by the equally offensive nude, *Olympia*, two years later. Monet had intended to submit his own version of a "Déjeuner sur l'Herbe" in 1866, but failed to complete it in time, so *Women in the Garden* was his first major attack on the citadel of the Salon.

The academic method of painting was essentially one of building form by means of tone. The painting was built on a lightly colored neutral ground, beginning with an underpainting of dark tones, usually brownish in hue. Into this dark underpainting the highlights were added in white or near-white, and the local color of the object or figure (its actual color) was introduced into the middle-toned areas. This method produced a strong sense of volume and solidity of form, but color played a secondary role, being diminished or sometimes even lost in highly illuminated or deeply shadowed areas. The method adopted by Manet, sometimes called *peinture claire*, was first to determine color areas through mid-tones and then to add highlights and darks into the wet paint, thus emphasizing shapes at the expense of form. This resulted in a strong color pattern, reminiscent of the then-popular Japanese prints, and also gave more importance to color itself, since the real colors of highlights and shadows could be given more consideration.

Monet went a stage further in this painting, giving a clear color identity to each shadow, such as that falling across the path and onto the dress of the seated figure. The resultant mauve-blue on the dress is one of the dominant colors in the work, and gives "uplift" to the tonal pattern. In the painting of the foliage there is a great variety of greens and yellows but no dark-toned shadows, and very little black is used, a color Monet was soon to abandon altogether.

The whole effect of the painting was thus antipathetic to standard academic practice, and the Salon judges were the reverse of artistically adventurous. The rejection, although undoubtedly disappointing for Monet, in no way deflected him from his chosen course.

Compositionally the painting is divided into quarters, pivoting on the springing of the branches of the small tree — an almost central spot in the work. The top half of the painting is in deep tone almost entirely occupied by foliage, while three or four figures, static and preoccupied, are concentrated in the left lower quarter. The moving figure is lit from the right and this light, falling across both the path and the dress of the seated figure, also strikes the flowers she is holding. The second bunch of flowers and flowering shrubs provide a moving ellipse through the outstretched arm, the lefthand figure, the skirt of the seated figure and across the path, giving a touch of animation.

The large scale of this work necessitated the digging of a trench into which the canvas was lowered to enable Monet to work on the top of the painting in the open air.

1

2

3

1 The foliage in this part of the painting is done in a variety of greens and brown with touches of black (Monet later abandoned the use of black). Some leaves are given emphasis with emerald green heightened with white and modified with yellow ocher, chrome yellow or cadmium yellow.

2 There is a curious quality about these two heads: the coyness of the eyes seen over the flowers and the pertness of the lefthand figure suggest that some dramatic relationship, or "story line," is intended, but nothing is explicit. The whole group is lower in tone, with these flowers quite muted in comparison with the others.
    Painted thickly and freely, the flowers provide an enlivening note of warm color in a part of the painting which is largely cool and shaded.

3 This is the liveliest piece of virtuoso brushwork in the whole painting, and reminds us that this large work was in part an advertisement of the artist's skill, designed to establish his ability at handling large-scale compositions. The cast shadow from the flowers is a delicate mauve-violet, a departure from the usual academic practice and the beginning of Monet's search for true color equivalents, as distinct from tones, in every part of a painting. The blue-mauve tint of the upper part of the dress, sharpened by the warm yellow-brown hat ribbon, a near complementary, provides a lively background.

4

4 *Actual size detail* The solid
blocked paint can be seen
clearly in this detail. The basis
for the color is probably burnt
sienna with white. The blue-
green halo effect heightens
the hair color, and the flesh is
treated in a grayish tone, as
deep as possible to retain the
head shape while still laying
emphasis on the hair.

BATHING AT LA GRENOUILLERE

1869

22×29in/56×73.5cm

Oil on canvas

Courtauld Institute Galleries, London

La Grenouillère was a popular bathing and boating place on the Seine close to Bougival, where Monet was living and working in 1869. During the 1860s it had become a weekend Mecca for Parisians who enjoyed the rural surroundings and the floating restaurant (to be seen in Monet's painting). Monet and Renoir often painted together at this time, producing different treatments of the same subject.

This painting, like *Women in the Garden*, shows the influence of Manet, who was something of a hero figure to the younger painters who were to become the Impressionists. (Manet, although an acknowledged leader of the avant garde, longed for an official recognition which never came.) In one respect, however, Monet's painting practice diverged from Manet's, as the latter painted in his studio from studies while Monet increasingly painted in the open air, directly from his subject. As he became more successful the need to exhibit at the Salon diminished and he painted no more large-scale, would-be "exhibition" pieces; the outdoor paintings were usually smaller in size and much more freely painted than studio works. The rather sketch-like treatment is an important characteristic of *La Grenouillère*, which is also quite small.

Monet used a number of terms to describe his studies, among them being: *esquisse*, which was a preliminary sketch or working drawing; *ébauche*, a rough oil sketch; *pochade*, which was another term for a sketch, more commonly applied to color-key design; *étude*, a part study to resolve some specific painting problem; and *croquis*, a rough draft. He used these words in a way slightly different from their usual meanings, but for Monet the distinctions were essential. He also employed two terms that were peculiar to him, one such being "impression," a word which he incorporated into the titles of several of his works. His other specialized and individual term, *enveloppe*, had an even more

precise meaning for him, and was used to describe the way an object was surrounded by light.

Bathing at La Grenouillère is not a highly finished work, the surfaces being quite rough in comparison with the fashionable Salon works. The brushstrokes are bold, broad and directional, often overlapping, with the paint used fairly wet (oily). The brushstrokes are highly descriptive, following forms and describing objects. For instance long horizontal strokes have been used for the shapes of the boats and long thin ones for the oars, while short dabs of color describe the foliage (top center). Even the human forms are drawn in flat, vertical strokes, and there is a good deal of overpainting with thick, wet paint, the figures on the duckboard being interspersed with thick strokes added later.

The composition is unconventional too. The duckboard divides the work horizontally almost across the middle, and this, with the vertical division running through the central dark foliage to the lower righthand boat, provides a quartered composition in which each quarter reflects a different character. The vertical access to the painting is emphasized by the almost central position of the dark figure on the duckboard, while in the lower half the broad shapes of the boats are a foil to the sparkling short strokes, blue and cool, used to describe the water. This in turn balances the warm colors in the upper half. The small skiff on the right is a later addition to provide a "stop" at the righthand edge, and the lefthand top segment gives enough color variety to balance both the boats below and the roughness of the group to the right. Although the painting is a direct study of the scene, the composition is as carefully calculated as that of a studio painting. Particularly interesting is the overhanging dark green foliage at the top center which comes forward to emphasize the picture plane, sending all the rest of the scene further back in space.

This is a very freely painted blocked-in sketch, clearly a direct study. Boldly divided across the middle by the duckboard walk, the lower half is in shadow and thus low in tone, while the upper contains the liveliest, most varied brushwork. Figures and objects are indicated by a few strokes of a paint-filled flat brush in which the color, although premixed, often carries traces of other colors which have remained on the brush.

1

1 *Actual size detail* The different layers of superimposed paint reveal the quick development of the sketch. Pulled over thick, dry paint a further thick mixture of blue-gray reveals the underpainting. Single brushstrokes indicate figures, while direct dabs of a round brush, leaving impasto dots and ridges, indicate foliage. Almost pure vermilion covers a mixture of viridian and chrome green in the bottom left, resulting in a heightened color contrast.

2 The most brilliantly lit quarter of the small canvas shows a small area of cobalt violet, a then recently invented opaque color. This is mixed with white alone to give a startling luminous quality of the distance. The dark figure in Prussian blue balances this whole rapidly laid-in light area. The brushstrokes are all designed to capture, quickly and directly, the immediate visual sensation, and form is subordinated to light and dark shapes, either contrasts or similarities.

3 Although the darkest area of the painting, the brushwork here is most carefully descriptive. The shapes and colors of the boats and their steep perspective treatment draw the viewer deeply into the scene. The foliage at the top, in mixtures of black, Prussian blue and chrome green or viridian, pushes the boats into a visual "funnel." Directional brushstrokes have been used to define the forms, a method Monet abandoned in his later work when the influence of Manet's technique diminished.

2

3

IMPRESSION, SUNRISE

1872

19×25in/48×63.5cm

Oil on possibly reused canvas

Musée Marmottan, Paris

This small painting has become one of Monet's most important works by virtue of the title he chose for it, and to fully understand Monet's work it is necessary to understand the significance the word "impression" had for him. One of the canvases submitted for the First Impressionist Exhibition in 1874, this was singled out by an antagonistic critic as typifying the "half-finished" look of all the works on show, and he dubbed the group "Impressionists."

In the personal terminology Monet used to describe his various types of paintings he would normally have called this work a *pochade* (sketch). However, as he said himself, he called it "impression" because "it really could not pass as a view of Le Havre," and he subsequently used the same word for a number of his paintings, all of them quick atmospheric sketches capturing a particular light effect. An "impression" for Monet was a special and limited form of sketch, and although the other Impressionists accepted the word as a reasonable description of their aims, Monet himself used it only when he felt it appropriate to a particular work.

Thus it appears that he did not really regard himself as an "Impressionist," and as a description of the diversity of aims of the other painters who exhibited in 1874 it hardly seems very revealing. However, it is the term universally adopted of the movement which became one of the most popular in the entire history of art, and is also frequently applied to painters — and even sculptors — only remotely connected with the original group.

Impression, Sunrise is a slight sketch, almost certainly completed on the spot in a single sitting, depicting the harbour at Le Havre as the sun rises over the cranes, derricks and masts of the anchored ships. The only evidence of life is the lazy action of the oarsman in the most sharply defined part of the painting. The painting gives a suggestion of the early morning mist, at that time clogged with the industrial smoke of the city, and has a strong relationship to the earlier views of mist and fog done in London in 1870. Monet had only recent returned from London, and his abiding impression of the city, recalled later, was of its fog. While there, he had seen the work of J.M.W. Turner (1775-1851), who is generally thought to have been an important influence on Monet and the other Impressionists, and he may also have seen some of the early *Nocturnes* by his contemporary Whistler.

At this time Monet was still painting scenes of urban and industrial life, though his vision was entirely that of a landscape painter and his interest mainly in the effects of light rather than in any specific architectural features or the social significance of the manifestations of industry. The most obvious characteristic of *Impression, Sunrise* is its immediacy of execution and the way it captures just one perceived instant. The forceful, clear shape and strong color of the sun provides the keynote for the work, with the dense, muted pale blue surrounding it providing the opposition of complementary colors which enhances the brilliance of both. The dark note of the nearest boat identifies and stabilizes the color key, the darkest element in the whole painting being the single near-black accented horizontal defining the waterline. With the passage of time, underpainting sometimes begins to come through, and here we can see some early drawing in the lower left- and righthand areas, further evidence of the urgency and immediacy of the painting.

The color character of this painting relies on the opposition of complementaries or near complementaries — orange and blue. In the top left a brown (a mixture of the same orange and blue) gives a linking color note. The composition, though simple, like that of most Impressionist paintings, is nevertheless dramatically effective. The indistinct forms of the port run across the canvas at Golden Section height, and a diagonal from the left edge through the three small boats emphasizes the positioning of the orange sun, while the middle small boat repeats the sun's position in the alternative quarter. The effect is a dynamic balance in which the reflection of the sun in the water contributes the enlivening element.

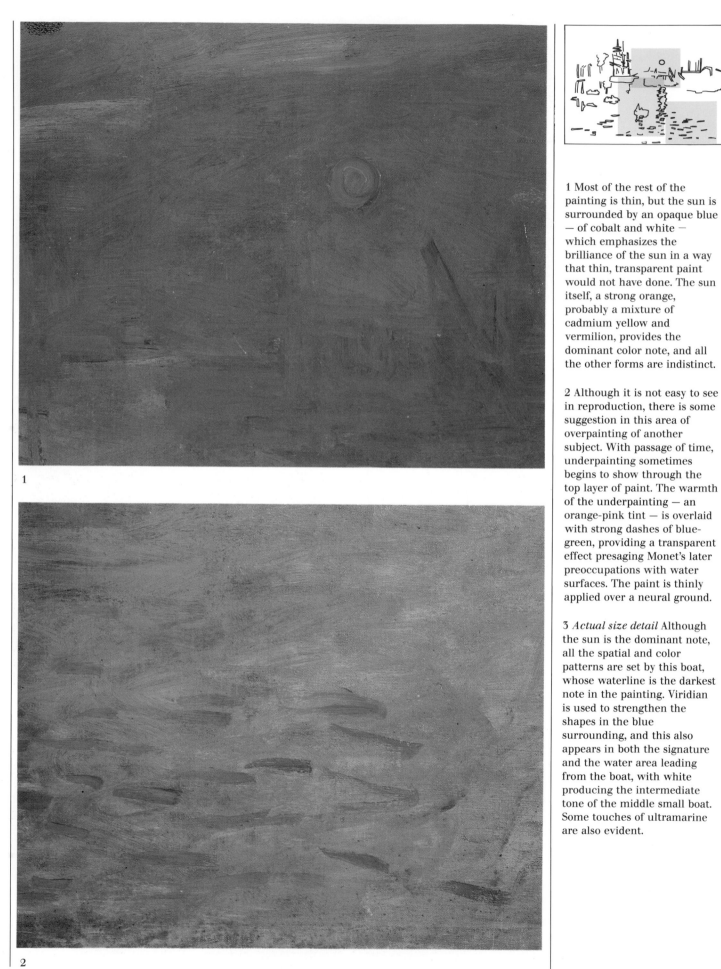

1

2

1 Most of the rest of the painting is thin, but the sun is surrounded by an opaque blue — of cobalt and white — which emphasizes the brilliance of the sun in a way that thin, transparent paint would not have done. The sun itself, a strong orange, probably a mixture of cadmium yellow and vermilion, provides the dominant color note, and all the other forms are indistinct.

2 Although it is not easy to see in reproduction, there is some suggestion in this area of overpainting of another subject. With passage of time, underpainting sometimes begins to show through the top layer of paint. The warmth of the underpainting — an orange-pink tint — is overlaid with strong dashes of blue-green, providing a transparent effect presaging Monet's later preoccupations with water surfaces. The paint is thinly applied over a neural ground.

3 *Actual size detail* Although the sun is the dominant note, all the spatial and color patterns are set by this boat, whose waterline is the darkest note in the painting. Viridian is used to strengthen the shapes in the blue surrounding, and this also appears in both the signature and the water area leading from the boat, with white producing the intermediate tone of the middle small boat. Some touches of ultramarine are also evident.

3 *Actual size detail*

AUTUMN AT ARGENTEUIL

1873

Oil on canvas

22×29in/56×75cm

Courtauld Institute Galleries, London

Monet's home at Argenteuil was his first really settled place since leaving the family house at Le Havre. With a new wife and a young son he needed a stable base, and his choice of Argenteuil gave him what proved to be some of his happiest years. Arriving in December 1871, when he had just turned thirty-one, he settled into the rented house near the railway bridge which formed the subject of a number of his paintings. During the next six years the countryside around Argenteuil and the town itself became the center for the development of the Impressionist movement, as his fellow-artists came out from Paris to work with him and to discuss their new ideas.

Monet's life at Argenteuil was more comfortable than is sometimes believed. He was beginning to sell his paintings and made a reasonable income — on a par with an office worker and about five times more than any local laborer. Dealers, too, visited him, particularly Durand-Ruel, and bought his work. Nevertheless, he was always short of money and often borrowed from his friends so that he could entertain them well.

Once settled, he painted with great enthusiasm, in the first year alone (1872) producing forty-six paintings, of which thirty-eight were sold. Most of these were views of the Seine, the town and the surrounding landscape; he had now changed from being a much traveled painter to being one who explored his own locality to the exclusion of all else.

Autumn at Argenteuil is typical of the lyrical painting technique he was developing to explore the light effects which excited him so much. This is a much more worked painting than *Impression, Sunrise*, and shows the new range of his oil-painting method. From the strong directional brushstrokes found in *Bathing at La Grenouillère* or the nervous delicate sketchiness of *Impression, Sunrise* Monet had now moved to a denser, more light-catching paint surface. Here the scene is shown bathed in the consistent and unified light that Monet believed should pervade every part of the painting and enclose it. He used the word *enveloppe* to describe this effect. It is difficult to define, but a comparison between this and *Bathing at La Grenouillère* (see page 23) makes it clearer. In the latter, each part seems to some extent separately painted, whereas in this painting there is total unity — it all seems to have come together under the all-pervading light.

As in many of Monet's paintings of water done at the time, the division between it and the sky is defined only by the strong blue horizontal which holds the delicate balance between the lefthand and righthand foliage forms. The darkest area, in ultramarine, on the righthand edge, is the hinge on which the painting sits — much as the dark line of the boat in *Impression, Sunrise* (see page 27) provides a spatial focus for the painting. There is also something of the same use of complementary colors, orange and blue, with the orange predominating, and there is opposition, or contrast, in the paint surface itself, with the broad areas of sky and water painted fluidly and the foliage done with dense dots of drier paint. It is interesting to see the change in painting technique between the actual foliage and its reflection. The foliage has a quality of solidity which in the slightly deeper color of the reflection is given a vertical floating look. The tall tree on the right reveals a further characteristic of Monet's method. The form is crossed by a number of dragged strokes made with the brush handle which slightly lighten the density of the form, an improvisation which shows a concern with effect rather than with traditional finish.

The mass of foliage on the left almost reaches to the center of the painting — the dark spire — and dominates, with its reflection, the left half of the work. A soft, almost amorphous shape, it contrasts with the sharper colors and more definite form of the tree on the right, the lower foliage on the right being indeterminately treated. Apart from the signature, the darkest tone is found, as a note of emphasis, on the middle right edge. The central section showing the town sits on a strong, thick blue line, stabilizing the whole composition. This line, although visually artificial, adds a sharp middle between water and sky, containing something of both.

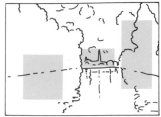

1

2

1 The main interest in this detail is perhaps the revealing fact that the density of paint in these distant features is the same as in the foreground, although recessive colors — blues and violets — have been used. This similar treatment of the paint surface over the whole picture has the effect of emphasizing unity, so that it is seen as a coherent painted surface rather than a depiction of space.

2 There is a marked difference in the paint surface of the trees and that of their reflections, although they are both heavily worked, thick paint. There is no precise division between foliage and water, but there is vertical smeared brushwork in the water area which is crossed by horizontal blue dashes which determine the surface, whereas the foliage itself is worked with close, stabbed brushstrokes. Monet's usual palette can be discerned in this detail. It included viridian, cadmium yellow, vermilion and cobalt blue, in mixture and with white. Some delicate vertical strokes of yellow-orange crossed by blue enliven this area — a characteristically Monet touch.

3 *Actual size detail* Monet's impasto technique, with overlay on overlay of dry dragged paint, is clearly revealed in this detail. Flecks of wet blue and cloud white suggest fluttering movement. The thick paint, which could have been too solid, is relieved by scoring into it with the handle of the brush so that the underpainting is revealed in places. The great number of colors used, from Prussian blue to vermilion, produce a characteristic density of effect.

3 *Actual size detail*

THE GARE SAINT-LAZARE

1877

29½×41⅓in/75×104.7cm

Oil on pale primed canvas

Musée d'Orsay, Paris

Saint Lazare station was the Paris railway terminus which served what might now be called "Monet country." It was the station not only for Argenteuil but also for most of Monet's favorite locations in northern France, including Le Havre, Chatou, Bougival, Louveciennes, Ville d'Avray, Rouen and Vernon (for the branch line to Giverny).

In 1876 Monet took a studio apartment in Rue Moncey close to the Gare Saint-Lazare, and from there, in 1877, between January and March, completed twelve paintings of the station. At this time he also had an apartment in the Rue d'Edinbourg, even closer to the station, so including his house at Argenteuil he actually had three residences. Evidently he was far from being poor.

As a group, these twelve paintings represent the last of his modern-life subjects, after which he turned completely to the natural landscape. The railway station was at that time the single most powerful reminder of the importance of industrialization to modern man, and a number of painters had treated the subject, the most emotive and romantic version being Turner's *Rain, Steam and Speed* of 1844. Turner had seen the train as a powerful force thrusting itself unfeelingly through a protesting nature, a dark and menacing beast, but Monet's train is very different — a delicate shape contained in an atmospheric web made of the intricate ironwork. His concern is with light and atmosphere, just as it would have been in a landscape of trees and water, but here they have been given a special character by the presence of the smoke and steam filtering the sunlight. The subject had an obvious fascination for a painter with his interests, and the fact that he made twelve paintings in such a short time is a testament to his enthusiasm. Another reason for his haste was that the wanted to include the paintings in the Fourth Impressionist Exhibition and the closing date was in April. In the event he exhibited only eight of the twelve. Once he had completed the group he seems to have been creatively exhausted, and only produced four other paintings that year.

Although they are a sequence of paintings, they are not, in Monet's terms of reference, a series, since they show a number of different views of the station rather than exploring the changing effect of light on the same view. The treatments vary from the oil-sketch to the studio-finished work, this painting having been done on the spot. He set up his painting stand centrally under the canopy, and the symmetricality of the composition is broken by both the large carriage shape on the left and the placing of the engine a little to the right of the center of the canopy of iron girders. The directional movement in the composition is provided by the movement toward the right of the foreground figure. Again, complementary colors have been used to enhance one another, this time the mauvish smoke and the pale yellow glowing sunlight, and the carefully constructed smoke pattern is both the whole color key and the element that gives life and rhythm to the work. The brushwork is no longer directional; it is a dense impasto laid on with such delicacy that even the harsh shape of the engine is softened into a steam-bathed form. The almost ethereal light makes the figures appear more as points of movement than as actual people going about their business.

This is a carefully constructed composition which avoids too much symmetricality by simple devices of balance and placing. Although the canopy is exactly central (reflecting Monet's painting position), the engine is a little to the left, and the bulky shape of the carriage and the direction of the smoke from the engine continue the emphasis on the left side of the painting. The framework of the side of the shed extends this further, while the right side is left open, filled with light sharpened by the small dabs of sharp color suggesting figures and objects. The general warmth of color is emphasized by the floating areas of steam and smoke in white and cobalt violet tints — at once exciting and surprising. As Monet's painting developed it became increasingly high in key until the time of the later water garden series (see pages 56-61), when the deep blues and greens returned, used with an even greater mastery.

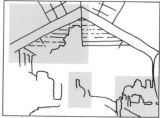

1

2

1 In this area Monet is accurate to an unusual degree, and the structure is clearly defined, providing a firm framework for the delicacy of the distant sunlit apartment buildings. The strong forms of the canopy are softened by the wisps of smoke which direct the eye to the dark engine smoke-stack.

2 This detail shows how roughly and sketchily the figures have been treated, with single blobs of flesh tint standing for faces and hands. The carefully placed pattern of dark brown and light red on the lefthand figure of a woman suggests the shape of the dress, but no precise description has been attempted.

3 *Actual size detail* The characteristic density of overpainting and the spatial implications it can acquire are very evident here. No form is precisely delineated but everything is seen, statically and in painterly terms. Although the brushstrokes are no longer form-following, as in *La Grenouillère*, each one nevertheless relates to form, for instance, the engine shape is specifically identified. The apparent use of black dryly overpainted on a dry underpainting is significant in suggesting Monet's desire for a deep, dark luminosity — he had not yet begun to reject the use of black on principle. The surrounding area, with orange and blue in lively conjunction, adds a forceful contrast.

3 *Actual size detail*

BOATS AT ETRETAT

1883

26 × 32in/66 × 81cm

Oil on canvas

Musée d'Orsay, Paris

Throughout his painting life Monet was fascinated by the effect of water. From his earliest seascapes at Le Havre and Trouville, inspired by his first mentors Boudin and Jongkind, to the last greater *Waterlilies* panels (see page 57) of his water garden at Giverny, he pursued his obsession with the surface of water. Its opaque restlessness in a choppy or rough sea, its reflectivity in strong sunlight, and its paradoxical non-presence in still dark ponds, all fascinated him. This is not surprising since the most constant concern of Monet and the other Impressionists was with the ever-changing surfaces in nature.

This is one of several paintings done between 1883-86 during visits to the cliff coast near Etretat, north of Le Havre. Unlike the later true "series" paintings, such as the *Grain Stacks* or the *Poplars,* where the same view was seen under different lights, Monet chose a variety of viewpoints and locations for the Etretat paintings.

During his first three-week visit in February 1883, he started but did not finish a number of paintings intended for an exhibition at Durand-Ruel's gallery in March. After a period of estrangement Durand-Ruel had again become Monet's dealer, but in the event Monet was unable (and unwilling) to supply any Etretat paintings for this show. This particular view was probably the one that was eventually taken by the dealer in 1886 after it had been further worked on in the painter's studio. There is a degree of finish in the foreground boats that suggests studio work.

The writer Guy de Maupassant, a valued friend of Monet's, stayed with him at Etretat in one of his visits in 1885 and he has left an interesting and revealing account of Monet's working methods at the time. "Off he went, followed by children carrying his canvases, five or six canvases representing the same subject at different times of the day and with different light effects. He picked them up and put them down in turn, according to the changing weather."

Etretat also had many artistic associations. Monet later owned a Delacroix watercolor of it; he knew Courbet's painting of boats on the beach there (one of his paintings used a similar composition) and Boudin had also used it as a subject. By 1883 Etretat had become a popular resort and, although Monet usually stayed later in the year after the Parisian trippers had left, he was nevertheless aware of its popularity with the Parisian public to whom, eventually, his paintings would be exhibited.

Fishing was an important means of livelihood all along the Normandy coast, a constant battle between the uncompromising power of the sea and the courage of the fishing folk with their small but sturdy boats, and this painting gives an impression of impending activity, with bustle on the beach and the sea choppy. The treatment of the hard forms of the boats, painted directionally as in *Bathing at La Grenouillère* (see page 25) is at variance with the looser, more atmospheric treatment of landscape and sea. It should also be noted that there is a curious inconsistency of scale in the painting: the boats on the right, whose size is established by the standing foreground figures, suggest that the two sailing boats on the left are very small indeed, while the figures in the middle distance seem out of scale with those in the foreground. The overall effect of this is to thrust the cliffs forward in the painting and to make the shore, as it approaches them, rather unconvincing. Altogether, although it may be possible to see what the artist's intentions were, the result is not completely convincing or unified.

The work is thinly painted on a pale-tinted primed canvas without, for the most part, the thick impasto of the earlier *Gare Saint-Lazare* or the later *Grain Stacks*. It is essentially a small open-air sketch with all the vibrant quality of direct observation. Compositionally it is rather unbalanced, the strength of the boat forms pulling to the right. A diagonal taken from the bottom left to the top right shows two different painting procedures, with that on the left being much looser and more luminous.

1 *Actual size detail*

1 *Actual size detail* The strength of this detail lies in the full colors — viridian, cobalt, ultramarine, vermilion and cadmium yellow combined with a dark near-black Prussian blue-vermilion mixture for the shapes and shadows. The strokes are form-shaping and directional, and the figures are indicated simply and with touches of near-white for emphasis. The unity of color is helped by the fact that the tinted ground has been allowed to show through in places.

2

2 The sea is painted quite thinly, with the warm, creamy tint of the canvas ground being allowed to show through. The red sails, their color echoing that of the foreground boats, are composed of just one or two rapid brushstrokes of vermilion, with a little darker red-brown blended in to suggest form.

Opposite page Monet painted a great many studies of Etretat and the coastal villages nearby. *The Sea at Fecamp* is essentially a sea study, the cliffs being sketched in without, it seems, great analytical interest, but the sea evidently carefully studied to create the feeling of the great Atlantic rollers as they follow each other in quick succession to break on the beaches. *Morning at Etretat*, taken from the same position as *Boats at Etretat*, and painted on a pale gray-tinted canvas, shows a different mood and treatment. A rougher, more changeable weather pattern with sunlight on the cliffs and shadows on the sea is treated in nervous, jerky brushstrokes. There is more overpainting on the left and the color contrasts in the water are stronger — viridian, Prussian and cobalt blues with touches of yellows.

The Sea at Fecamp 1881, Private collection

Morning at Etretat 1883, Private collection

GRAIN STACKS, END OF SUMMER

1890/1

$23\frac{3}{4} \times 39\frac{1}{4}$ in/60×100 cm

Musée d'Orsay, Paris

Once Monet had settled at Giverny with Alice Hoschedé he had a firmly established base from which, during the last years of the 1880s, he was able to make extended painting trips to other locations.

In 1890 he began a series of local paintings which marked an important stage in his development and which he himself regarded as a turning point. He continued to undertake occasional painting excursions in France and abroad, but from this time on the focus of his work, as of his life, was Giverny.

In the field facing his studio window there was a group of grain stacks from which he made his first true series paintings. Although these are frequently described as haystacks they are in fact stacks of grain or corn — the basic livelihood of the local people. In the hands of another painter, François Millet for example, these might have had a social or symbolic significance, but for Monet they were bulky indefinite forms whose structure, loose undefined shapes and varied light and color effects provided a marvelously appropriate model for his preoccupations.

For Monet the decision to paint a series came as a fresh and exciting new direction, refocusing his work from subject painting to the expression of a surrounding, ever-changing, all-embracing light revealed through color. It was not the grain stacks themselves that held the intrinsic interest for him, but the light that revealed them and the atmosphere that surrounded them. His main preoccupation, the quick changes in light effect that he encountered as he painted, had now also become his main problem. Each perceptible change really demanded a new painting since the real subject was "instantaneity" itself. The only solution, he concluded, was to do a series of paintings each from the same spot but at different times of the day. The changes in light and color were so frequent that he evolved a method of working on a number of paintings each day,

returning to them in rotation on subsequent days when the light was exactly right. This, not unnaturally, caused him to have frequent outbursts of rage and frustration when the weather failed to co-operate.

This first series resulted in over thirty paintings, all completed between the summer of 1890 and May 1891 when fifteen of them were exhibited in a one-man show at Durand-Ruel's gallery. Monet had originally intended to show only the *Grain Stacks* series, but at the last moment he included a number of other subjects. The success of the show probably strengthened his determination to continue the series paintings.

This first series was followed by several others and, as with Turner before him, light became his master. It was when he was working on these paintings that he said: "For me, a landscape does not exist in its own right since its appearance changes at every moment; but its surroundings bring it to life — the air and the light which vary continuously." And again: "the *motif* is an insignificant factor; what I want to reproduce is what lies between the *motif* and me." Painting became a constant struggle with change — "the sun moves so quickly I can't keep up with it." And indeed he could not. Before he sent these paintings to his exhibition he worked on them, retouching them in his studio to strengthen the qualities of light and atmosphere.

This later studio working can be seen in the *Grain Stacks* paintings, in many of which the *pentimento* (the "ghost" of an old form showing through the new) and the dense, almost consistently textured impasto, particularly where the forms meet the sky, indicate the extent of his struggles. In his earlier paintings the treatment is direct and, although there is sometimes considerable overpainting, it comes from fresh vision insights, whereas in the *Grain Stacks* the surface of the canvas has become almost a battlefield of "instantaneity."

One of the last of the summer *Grain Stack* series, this one begins to show the first signs of autumn mists. The cobalt blue tint in the distant upland and the warm gray of the sky suggest a thick atmosphere that will in time roll down to cover the whole landscape, first the bright green trees and then the grain stacks themselves.

There is an interesting difference in tonal character between the two stacks. The more distant smaller stack is in a darker, muddier color with a viridian/Prussian blue cast shadow; the other is more luminous, and with the mauve and cobalt blue shadowed areas lighter in tone. The usual tonal treatment is therefore reversed.

1 In this detail the density of overpainting and the constant reworking to produce a shimmering atmospheric evening light of blue luminosity over the backing upland can be clearly seen. The free working of the trees in bright green and yellow adds the sharp touch which emphasizes the effect of warm color in the drying grain stacks, with wet paint in blue-gray drawn over a warm ocher-colored underpainting.

2 This shadow and sunlight area clearly shows the range of Monet's colors. The mauve and cobalt blue used for the stack appears again in the shadow, which is enlivened by touches of the warm oranges and greens used for the sunlit patch in front.

1

2

3

3 *Actual size detail* The grain stacks were painted rapidly, largely on the spot — during the course of one day Monet worked on several paintings successively. There is thus a great deal of wet paint overlaying the lower impasto as well as some fluid overpainting in the last stages.

Sometimes the paintings were finished or reworked in the studio. In this detail the warm underpainting of the stack itself has blue-violet thin paint partially covering it, which was probably added later. The touches of viridian and yellow are also probably studio embellishments.

POPLARS ON THE BANKS OF THE EPTE

1891
$39\frac{3}{4} \times 26$in/101×66cm
Oil on canvas
Private collection

After his first Giverny series of *Grain Stacks*, with their bulky, solid forms, Monet chose a linear subject — a row of poplar trees by the side of a small river. The delicate tracery of foliage around the sharp vertical lines of the trunks and the strong horizontal emphasis of the river bank gave him the opportunity for new exercises in light. Here his *enveloppe* presented a new and exciting challenge; there was more air and sky than solid form.

Monet found the poplars marked for felling and paid their owner to leave them standing until he had finished painting them. He started in July 1891 and worked on the paintings until October, choosing mainly afternoon and evening effects, with the light falling from the right. The weather was poor at Giverny that year, and Monet, always bad-tempered when prevented from painting, became frustrated and irascible, fearing also that the trees would have to be felled before long. He complained about "this appalling weather which makes me fear for my trees."

As with his other series, he worked on a number of canvases during the same painting session, moving from one to the other as the light changed. His speed of working is astonishing: he allowed himself only seven minutes on one of the poplar paintings — "until the sunlight left a certain leaf," were his own words.

The compositions are generally of two types. The first is a vertical pattern of bars — created by the trunks — opposed to the single horizontal of the river bank, usually placed low on the canvas with the reflections carrying the line of the trunks right down through the horizontal. The second, as in this painting, takes the form of a single sweeping zigzag of foliage set against the sometimes broken verticals of the tree trunks. Here again the river bank provides a firm horizontal, and both foliage and tree-trunks are continued in the reflection.

The pictorial effect, very unusual and often very dramatic, emphasizes a characteristic which was to become a significant element in Monet's influence on later painting. It demands a positive effort of visual interpretation to turn the dramatically effective pattern of a painted surface into acceptable three-dimensional representation of a particular landscape. Because the surface is so insistent, the painting tends to thrust forward instead of receding in space. The consciousness of surface, of the paint texture rather than illusionist space, is so much a part of twentieth-century pictorial consciousness that it is easy to forget the importance of Monet and the Impressionists in the formation of this concept. The poplar series is much concerned with space, and this element is very evident.

Poplars on the Banks of the Epte was probably painted in the flat evening light, the time when the direct sun has left the scene but dusk has not yet begun to remove the color. We cannot be sure of this, as the time of day is not indicated in the title as sometimes it is, but there is a very closely related painting in Philadelphia which is clearly in full sunlight, and it is likely that this version was painted soon afterward.

Monet's signature, which he came to consider a significant part of his paintings, is in red, which echoes the red on the tops of the trees and provides a balancing note at the base. The signature here is used as an element in the composition rather than being an "advertising" feature, as it is in *Women in the Garden* (see page 19).

The whole series of poplar paintings was exhibited at Durand-Ruel's gallery in February 1892 — the only one of Monet's exhibitions which was devoted to a single series. This painting was included and was brought to what Monet considered "exhibition standard" by later work in his Giverny studio. Durand-Ruel was quite firm with Monet in insisting on the need for "finish."

This is one of several treatments of the same view of trees, one of which shows more of the linear direction of the trees as they follow the bends of the river. Monet must have been interested in the criss-crossing of the lines as they receded along the banks to provide a pattern of receding tones and tints with a consequent loss of detail and narrowing range of tone. All these elements are to be discerned in this work, and particularly evident is the change of tone where the near bank meets the distant foliage.

On the lower right the deep Prussian blue and viridian in the bank are thrust forward by the warm area, enlivened by touches of vermilion. This is the darkest and most intense area of the painting, and the foliage appears almost to float away from it.

1

2

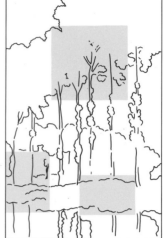

1 There is a delicate energy and visual delight in this area. Monet's experience in painting leaves in fluttering movement at differing times of the day enabled him to tackle this in a way that suggests enthusiasm and pleasure. Though the paint is solidly opaque, it is not heavily worked and contains flecks of many colors, deftly placed. The thin trunks of the poplars, although giving a strong vertical emphasis to the painting, are also delicately painted.

2 The density of overpainting, done in sharp, nervous, directional strokes, suggests that the resolution of this area of the painting presented the greatest difficulty. The waterline is not precise, and the bank must have been in deep shadow. The relationship of the enshrouding *enveloppe* of light with the freely painted upper area must have given problems.

3 *Actual size detail* A surprisingly separate detail — another tree or group of trees, standing apart from the poplar row, casts its reflection in the water. The color range is strongest here: bright blue-green (cobalt and viridian tints) provides a complementary balance for the strong if amorphous yellow-orange shape of the tree form and also for its darker reflection. This is painted with crossing horizontal and vertical brushstrokes expressing the water surface.

3 *Actual size detail*

ROUEN CATHEDRAL:
HARMONY IN BLUE AND GOLD

1893/4
42×28¾in/107×73cm
Oil on canvas
Musée d'Orsay, Paris

The series of paintings of the west front of Rouen Cathedral on which Monet worked during a number of visits in 1892 and 1893 are among the most important and revealing in his entire *oeuvre*. They show his full maturity as a painter, his command of technique, and his devotion to the series method of subject treatment. His ability to translate his vision into paint and his understanding of the nature of his own art were all established in front of this massive, gray, sculptured structure.

Although, as he said when he was painting the *Grain Stacks* series (see page 45), he was not so much concerned with the *motif* as what lay between the *motif* and him, the cathedral itself probably did have some emotional significance for him. The critics of the time certainly believed that this was so, and in a strongly Catholic country any subject even remotely connected with religion inevitably carries some overtones. Monet was painting at a time when Symbolism, as a literary and an art movement, was very much in vogue, and one critic went so far as to suggest that the closed doors of the west portal in Monet's painting symbolized Man's exclusion from the spiritual world. One might speculate as to whether Monet's own rejection of the Church might have had a bearing on his choice of subject. Certainly there are grounds for the theory that in these paintings Monet was looking for some extra dimension, since he was reported as telling a friend, while he was working in Rouen, that he was looking for "more serious qualities."

Most of the *Rouen* series are of the west front of the cathedral, showing most of the central portal and part or most of the tower situated to the left. They are all fully worked paintings with thick encrusted impasto surfaces, which in some cases have been subjected to drastic overpainting in colors varying considerably from the under-painting. Most, if not all, have been further worked on in the studio at a later date; the majority of them are dated 1894, the year after his last visit to Rouen. There is even a suggestion that some were entirely constructed in Monet's Giverny studio much later in his life. A friend of his, the painter Berthe Morisot, visited him after his last trip to Rouen and listed twenty-six Rouen paintings as the complete count, but at least thirty are now known. If there is truth in this implication it provides another interesting insight into Monet's attitude. We have already seen that the subject may have become more important to him than he intended, and now another of his tenets, that of *plein air* painting (giving the impression of open air by painting on the spot), seems also in question. The essence of Monet's painting and the genesis, at least in part, of the idea of series painting was his obsession with capturing the immediacy of light and atmosphere. The idea of retouching in the studio seems to contradict Monet's purpose, and the construction of a painting entirely from experience and visual memory was quite contrary to his own words. Part of the explanation for this seeming contradiction may lie in Monet's increasing success. The demands for his work were ever-growing and it is probable that in order to meet them successful *pochades* (sketches) were worked on and unsuccessful beginnings reworked in the studio, to be completed when an exhibition was imminent.

In this series Monet's major concern was with the possibilities of painting a heavy, static, large-scale sculptured form in the shape of a flat plane, on which the intricate architectural details were thrown into high relief as the light moved across it. The local (actual) color of the building is a dull gray, but in the paintings the light gives the color, almost dematerializing the forms themselves in the embracing *enveloppe* of atmosphere.

The whole painting
The title of this painting recalls Whistler's *Nocturne, Blue and Gold*, and suggests similar preoccupations; Monet knew Whistler and admired his work. Sunshine and shadow are suggested, and the heavily worked canvas also washes into white those areas not dominated by blue or golden yellow. As is often the case with Monet's paintings, the darkest area is located on the edge, in this instance at bottom right. This pulls the righthand side toward the picture plane, giving a recessive angle to the façade and a steep perspective slant to the roof line, adding a sense of movement to the heavy, solid form. The other two darker areas, the doorway and the circular west window recesses, contain within them the strongest colors, the most intense blue and gold. The shadows are consequently suffused with light and color, which washes out to the color from the full sunlight, and the whole painting is in a high key.

1 Comparison of this detail with the right side shows a marked difference in treatment. While on the right side the paint is, as usual, thickly and dryly applied, the left side suggests smooth pale overpainting with thin wet paint. The effect is to draw the left side into recession, focusing interest on the central portion. The brownish gray overpainting suggests a mixture of white with a little vermilion and cobalt.

2 The clock over the central doorway features in most of the cathedral series. Here the sharp red dot is almost exactly central, and with the cadmium yellow and near white, marks the brightest focus point in the painting. Its form is emphasized by the Prussian blue which surrounds it. The heavily worked paint, thickly encrusted, may well have been reworked in the studio later.

3 *Actual size detail* This detail reveals the thick, crusty paint characteristic of the *Rouen* series. Dry impasto is overlaid with touches of bright color. The yellows (probably cadmium) and the browns (probably gold ocher with some cadmium yellow) create the sunlight effect on a near white paste. The blues, violets and mauves using both cobalt and ultramarine tints are complementary to the yellows and give a luminosity to the shadows. Although forms seem indistinct the architectural structure is carefully maintained.

1

2

3 *Actual size detail*

MORNING WITH WILLOWS

One panel of the *Décoration des Nymphéas (Waterlily Decorations)*
1916-26
6ft 8in×42ft 6in/2m 3cm×12m 95cm
Musée d l'Orangerie, Paris

After his second wife Alice's death in May 1911, Monet was distraught and unable to work, shunning his friends and even losing interest in his garden. He was close to despair, which was exacerbated by concern for his failing eyesight, shortly to be diagnosed as caused by a double cataract. Although by the end of the year he had begun to paint again, he seemed to feel none of the dedication and purpose that had typified him in the past. When his son Jean died in 1914 at the age of forty-seven Monet became almost a recluse, his only human contact being with his friend Clemenceau and Blanche, Jean's widow, who cared for him until his death.

Clemenceau, at this time Prime Minister and in charge of the French war effort, still managed to find time to support and encourage Monet and to give him a new enthusiasm which carried him through the last decade of his life. Clemenceau persuaded Monet to reconsider an idea that the artist had projected earlier — for a series of large mural-sized water landscapes. Monet financed this project through the sale of old works; he had few newly painted canvases to sell since he had produced very little for the previous three years. He had a large new studio designed and built especially for the project (although with the shortage of labor caused by the war it was not completed until 1916.) Although Monet disliked the look of this huge, factory-like structure in his idyllic garden setting he nevertheless worked in it on the *Waterlilies* panels for the next ten years. The work tormented him; at moments he felt like destroying everything he had done and starting again, while at others he was buoyed up by the success of his efforts. He painted and repainted, employing thick impasto underpainting and thin wet overpainting; he spent hours in contemplation and then worked either furiously or steadily for short periods. He felt he had never completed the paintings and that he never would, but nevertheless they became an ever-deeper expression of his vision.

Although he had concentrated on waterlilies and the water garden since 1905 these panels marked a new departure for Monet. Firstly they extended horizontally to provide a much wider field of vision than he had considered before, and secondly they were on a much larger scale than anything he had previously attempted. These two factors alone might have daunted even an energetic young

painter, but Monet was old and his eyesight was poor and failing.

But the problems were not only physical and emotional. Much later Walter Sickert (1860-1942) expressed the view that Monet had "yielded to a fatal enlargement of scale that called for the strictest limitations of area." What he meant was that the paintings were on a huge scale while the subject — the surface of the water in his own water garden — was not. There are twelve panels, all exploring the same subject, this one alone being over six feet high and over forty-two feet long. No other large mural project in the history of art has attempted such concentration on one limited subject.

Sickert's comment gives rise to the question of whether the scale is actually too large for the content. Monet's obsession with water surfaces, particularly those he observed in his own water garden, can possibly be seen in the last analysis as a program of decoration, more of a record of obsession than a progressively renewing sense of discovery. Even so, the achievement is immense. No one can be in the presence of these panels without a feeling of spiritual enlargement as well as a pure physical delight in the paint surface and color. The very presence of the works is affecting and their scale is such that no reproduction can really convey their atmosphere.

The paint quality contributes enormously to the feeling of this floating world, as consisting of points of light over a varying blue depth; dense overpainting combines with lightly drawn-on color to pull the eye across the surface with constant pleasure. What is so captivating is the paradox of flat depth; the consciousness of the painting surface, mentioned earlier, here becomes palpable.

Monet donated these panels to the nation by an agreement signed in 1922 and they were placed in the Orangerie in 1927, a few months after his death. He never believed that he had finished them.

The subject matter of these panels is a panorama of the water surface of Monet's water garden, and the color consists for the most part of cool blues, greens and deep mauves, given heightened value by the luminous yellows and pinks and by the flowers picked out in sharp contrast. Monet saw the whole decoration as a continuous horizontal for a circular room.

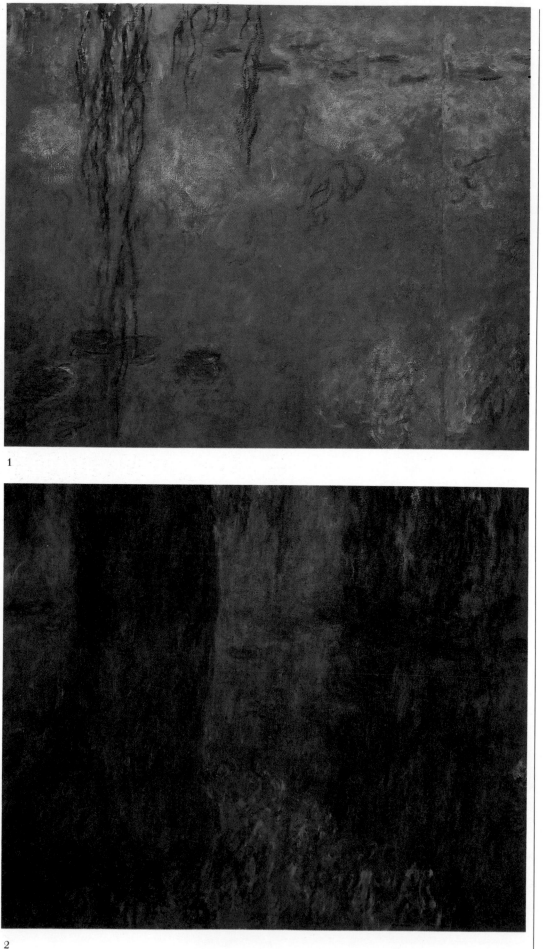

1

2

1 "The essence of the motif is the mirror of water whose appearance alters at every moment thanks to the patches of sky that are reflected in it, and which give it light and movement." This detail exemplifies Monet's comment, suggesting the sky within the water, sunlit with roseate clouds. Painted with thick paint in large action strokes and delicate touches, it expresses the controlled mastery achieved after a lifetime of experience.

2 The predominating paint quality of Prussian blues, ultramarine and viridian, mixed in the light areas with white, is balanced by the introduction of warm browns on the trunk of the tree and points of sharp yellow in the grasses. The deep, almost mysterious, shadowed water thrusts the bright green bank into prominence. It is part of the marvelous coherence of these panels that this balance of strong vertical notes and floating and amorphous areas of rich color is maintained in a moving balance throughout the whole project.

3 *Actual size detail* This detail of a single waterlily flower painted in sharp color in a dense impasto pigment gives, by implication, an insight into the great physical tenacity Monet showed in the production of these immense panels. When one reflects that this work was carried over hundreds of square feet of densely painted canvas, with layers of overpainting and repainting one can only be amazed at Monet's physical and mental reserves.

3 *Actual size detail*

4

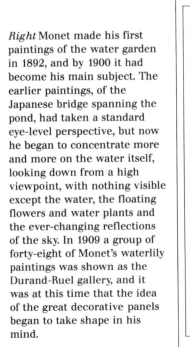

4 The floating indeterminate surface is thrust into its proper relationship with both the edges and the picture plane by the use of solid forms either in the water or on the banks. In this detail the falling fronds of weeping willow send the cloud reflection into a steep perspective recession which is brought back to the water surface through the use of dark and strong color on the lower edge.

Waterlilies, 1908

Right Monet made his first paintings of the water garden in 1892, and by 1900 it had become his main subject. The earlier paintings, of the Japanese bridge spanning the pond, had taken a standard eye-level perspective, but now he began to concentrate more and more on the water itself, looking down from a high viewpoint, with nothing visible except the water, the floating flowers and water plants and the ever-changing reflections of the sky. In 1909 a group of forty-eight of Monet's waterlily paintings was shown as the Durand-Ruel gallery, and it was at this time that the idea of the great decorative panels began to take shape in his mind.

Waterlilies, 1919

INDEX